Becoming A Seriously Happy Special Needs Mom

21 Steps to Finding Your HAPPY Place

Linda James Bennett

Publishing services provided by:

 **Archangel Ink**

ISBN-13: 978-1535538442
ISBN: 1535538449

Disclaimer

Preface

'There are only two ways to live your life. One is as though nothing is a miracle. The other is as though everything is a miracle.'

~ Albert Einstein

You are in the right place if you are a special needs mom and you agree with more than one of these statements:

- You feel like you're stuck and you want to make a positive change.
- You don't want to be secretly irritated by your Facebook friends anymore.
- You wish your friends and family were more compassionate.
- You wish you didn't feel so alone.
- You live with anxiety and fear about the future.

Good News! You are closer to being a seriously happy special needs mom than you think.

As I listen to special needs moms talk about how draining their lives are, I remember my early years. I didn't have the necessary inner resources to draw upon; instead, I turned to paid counselors and psychologists to help me understand and cope, just as you do today. Years later, I look around and I wonder where all the books about being a happy special needs mom are. Why doesn't someone talk about our health and well-being? Surely, the welfare of the special needs moms is important. Books about raising children with disabilities are readily available, but what about the parents? We need books that shine the light on the necessary coping skills required to be thriving special needs parents.

As special needs parents, we have more to sort through than the average parent does when it comes to emotional and psychological issues. Our kids are people with the same wants and needs as other children. Yet when it comes to helping our children achieve their goals, there are often steep mountains in our path.

Raising a child with special needs is a life full of responsibilities. We encounter situations that we would never have imagined in our wildest dreams. While you and I live with diverse circumstances, we all face the same bittersweet times in our lives. We share a common link.

We are here to talk about our happiness as special needs moms. I describe myself as *seriously* happy because I take my happiness very seriously – *now*. While Disneyland calls itself "The Happiest Place on Earth," I can't depend on my visits there for my happiness. It has to start as my daily routine. It has to be a priority in my life.

Other experienced special needs parents have achieved personal happiness while supporting their children. They have helped their children reach the level of independence they desire, but this does not happen by accident. We have chosen to be happy in the midst of our circumstances and you can, too.

This is my happiness journey. It all began when I realized that I wasn't very happy. I allowed my circumstances to steal my joy. Worst of all, I was oblivious to it.

My son Ryan often asks, "Mom, are you happy?" and then he wants me to ask him the same question. His reply, "Only when I have to be," used to annoy me because it seemed like such a silly remark. One day it finally hit me and I started thinking, *am I happy*? Do I just put on my happy face when I'm around others, making an effort to be light-hearted, and then turn it off when I get home? I didn't realize I was contributing to my state of grumpiness. Does this sound familiar?

So how did I change it up? The bottom line is becoming self-aware, self-conscious. I had to achieve a state of enlightenment, where I *chose* to be happy and joy-filled.

After allowing my life circumstances to beat me up, I learned how to turn it around through my Life Lessons. I want to share these lessons with you as tips, advice, and information for your success. They include lessons I learned about love, marriage, family, relationships, and myself.

Learning how to work through my doubts, special needs grief, and anxiety taught me to be fearless. I'm now facing my fears to be bold for my family's sake.

This book is not about my son's progress, or how we navigate the bureaucracy, or the absurd time-management issues we all share. This story is about my personal transformation from a drained and overwhelmed mom to a productive professional, caring friend, and grateful mother and wife. I realized how important it is to build strong positive connections with family and friends in creating my happy place. We all crave that connection—and yes, approval—from others, and those pats on the back that give you the confidence to keep going. Even better than a pat on the back from others is the one you give to yourself, when you need it most for a job well done.

My approach comes from many years of personal experiences of what worked for me and what didn't work at all. Learning this for yourself offers you more happiness and wealth in all areas of your life. This book will help you find what works for you.

Our family has remained together through all the trials of parenting two different kids with opposite destinies. We managed to find happiness with each foot securely planted in different worlds. I want the same accomplishment for you.

Here is what you can expect in this book: I have included my real-life examples, as well as my "fly on the wall" observations of other moms' struggles and triumphs over the years. Since we don't live in a bubble, some of my insights do apply to both the special needs and typical moms.

This book is not about religion. It is about my relationship with Jesus as my ultimate go-to counselor. You'll find that I give credit for my transformation to my "higher power" more than I do to my own efforts. I take enormous comfort knowing that I'm not in charge. For those of you that don't believe in Jesus or God, I can't imagine where you find your comfort. I know other moms who are angry with God for their life circumstances. If that is how you feel, I hope you will stay with me long enough to find value in the Life Lessons that I'm sharing.

Why Are Special Families Different?

Every family with an exceptional child is special. Our son Ryan changed our family, and I finally learned to trust God's plan and purpose. I discovered happiness, even as an imperfect woman, mother, and wife.

My story is much like the countless other moms parenting children with disabilities. We continue on this same path with our heads held high and with smiles on our faces. We have all accepted that we must be persistent and patient. We acknowledge that our children are blessings in our lives. We have learned to make lemonade out of the lemons thrown our way.

Sadly, I still struggle to be politically correct. After all these years, I have to stop and think what the politically correct way to describe my son is. One, I don't think of him as disabled, just a person. Second, I'm not happy that I have to describe him in a particular way that doesn't offend others. I must say that I have a child with special needs instead of saying that I have a special needs child. When Ryan was younger, these weren't the descriptions used. (I understand that the focus is on the child as a person first and they are not a disability.) Ryan doesn't care either way. Other people have changed my language. And I'm sure that it will certainly change again.

I wondered how I could give other special needs moms hope, encouragement, or a heads-up for the unnecessary potholes ahead. I kept thinking about writing this book. This book is for moms, because as a mom, this is what I know. While my husband, John, is a key player in all this, this book isn't for or about "the dads." This book is self-serving; it is all about moms and their day-to-day struggles to survive in the face of anger, confusion, and anxiety. I find that dads are often thrown under the bus because as moms we can't let go of our kids. I wish *every* child had both parents under the same roof. But, that is not possible, and so I'm here for "the moms."

This book is about how to take care of YOU, how to heal YOU, and how to protect YOU while you are caring for your special child.

Welcome to the Exceptional Parent's Place. I'm excited to have you with me. Grab a cup of coffee, get comfortable, and let's get started.

A final note: Check out the FREE bonuses materials I created to help you at www.ExceptionalParentsPlace.com/BonusMaterials

Contents

Introduction

'We must accept finite disappointment but never lose infinite hope.'

~ Martin Luther King, Jr.

Hi, I'm Linda James Bennett. I've been married to John over forty years. We have two sons: our first Ryan is intellectually disabled and our second Christopher is considered typical (or as most people would say, normal). I'm writing to give you hope, encouragement, and to guide you back to your Happy Place.

Life in the special needs world is scary, lonely, and overwhelming at first. If you're like me, you're even scared yourself. I have cried thinking about my son's future when he is alone in the world. What will happen to him without me to protect him? What will become of him? I'm sure you know what I mean. I remind myself that I have to stop the negative thinking about a bleak, hopeless future for my son, while at the same time working diligently to try to change it.

Maybe you have felt like an outsider in a group of moms who are naturally bragging about their typical child. These same moms can't imagine what it is like to parent a child with special needs for *the rest of their lives*. Like all parents, we want a lifetime of happiness for our kids and pray that we will live long enough to see it happen. To cope with these feelings, I have learned to compartmentalize my heartache. I secure them in a little box with a tight-fitting lid, tucked away on a hard-to-reach shelf in my mind. Now I can focus on the job at hand—living and enjoying life.

Before children, my husband and I were living the carefree lifestyle. Our biggest responsibilities were taking care of a cat, and then a dog for six years before our first son, Ryan came along. We were living the dream. We expected more of the same for all our children. Sound familiar?

I savored all the baby books that told me what to expect from pregnancy, and how to care for your typical baby. It was fun and exciting getting ready for the big day. What I didn't read was what to expect when you have a child with special needs, because that book didn't exist. Where was the book to help me with the emotional journey that I was about to experience? The book that would prepare me for the changes this baby would have on our lives.

My son was slow to reach all his developmental milestones. My hope had been that he would catch up with all the other kids in school. We thought with therapy it could change. We turned to DNA testing to determine why he was different. When we received the results, we realized that wasn't going to happen. We are lifetime members of the special needs world.

Living in the special needs world was different from the life my friends and family were experiencing. I began to see and feel the changes immediately. While everyone else was traveling down the common road, we found ourselves on the alternate path. The path was full of people, places, and practices we never could have imagined, and it meant leaving behind the life I had prepared for. Without our anchors to count on for advice and guidance (such as my mommy friends or our family) John and I had to find our way on our own.

We all share similar frustrations as we try to find our way. It affects everything we do. All the typical choices are no longer the right solution. It becomes the undercurrent of our life. Our frustrations are like the pink elephant in the room, they're always there, but we don't talk about them. The question is how do we cope with this?

Disappointments were everywhere when I compared my life to my friends. They appeared to be floating along while I felt like I was constantly swimming upstream. All these negative feelings build over time and, left unchecked, will develop into negative behaviors. Depression, anger, isolation, and conflict will become your new point of view.

Guess what... we aren't in Kansas anymore (as Dorothy in the Wizard of Oz would say). I had to adapt to our new life or I was at risk of drowning. It became clear that I had to deal with all these issues to enjoy my life.

If I couldn't have the life my friends had, then maybe I could still have a good life, but on different terms.

I realized that being a special needs parent is more than raising a special child. It is also about taking care of YOU along the way. I had become so laser-focused on our son that I forgot about my own joy. I have seen many special needs moms fall into the same trap. You believe that if you don't do everything possible for our child, they will not thrive. Say hello to the "Helicopter Mom"—a mom who hovers over their child, fearing one misstep will lead to disaster. One helicopter mom I know restricts her child from personal growth opportunities because of her anxieties. You wear yourself out trying to control their lives. I believe my responsibility is to teach my son to be as independent as he can be, to thrive without me.

While we need to do everything possible for our child, the special needs mom must have a life of her own. To be happy we need to expand ourselves to be all that we were created to be. Not a one-note wonder, but a full symphony of sights and sounds.

Consider this wisdom by comedian Jeff Foxworthy: 'I know that if mama ain't happy, ain't nobody happy.'

Help, Something Is Wrong With My Child

'Ask, and it will be given you. Seek, and you will find. Knock, and it will be opened for you.'

~ Matthew 7:7-8WEB

Every mom is thinking about the health of their child from the moment they find out that they are expecting. Me too. I wanted to do everything possible to bring a healthy baby into the world. When I gave up coffee, I wondered how in the world I was going to function without my daily dose of caffeine to get me going. Out the window went the relaxing glass of wine after work. Then came those huge neonatal vitamins that looked like horse pills. I was all-in for this pregnancy and willing to give up or do whatever I needed to do to have a healthy child.

From the moment I felt my baby move I was naturally curious about how and what he or she was doing inside my belly. Aren't we all that way? How did the baby look and was it a boy or a girl? I was so excited at twenty-six years old to become a mom, convinced that nine months was too long to wait. Six would have been much better. My life was about to change, and I was ready to discover the wonders of this new miracle—our baby.

With the new baby, my fairy tale dream was coming to life. I had an exciting career, a marriage to my ideal man, a big extended family, kids, a dog, and a home. But the story was about to take a different twist and turn.

Like all parents, we were expecting a healthy child. After a normal birth, we thought we were in the clear. All parents want to share their remarkable baby milestones with others. How their child was rolling over, walking, or talking at such an early age. But, that was not our story. We started asking questions like why wasn't he on schedule like the other babies? We noticed that Ryan was in the lower percentile for his developmental milestones.

What was happening?

As new parents, our intuition, or *parent radar system* started alerting us to problems. "Something isn't right…" so we began asking questions and then more questions. The answers were frustrating or insufficient. I insisted that there must be a reason why he had all these problems. I expected the doctors to have all the answers.

I remember thinking that this was not part of my plan. I learned the only choice I had was to keep putting one foot in front of the other. We had to keep looking for solid explanations, and praying that we were on the right track.

We Have A Decision To Make……..

While watching Ryan at Sea World playing and laughing one day, I wondered how he saw the world. I imagined putting on magical Ryan glasses to try to understand his world. What did it look like? Was it just like other typical children? As I watched him interact with the people around him, it occurred to me that life *was* simple to him. I realized that despite the "labels" others had given him, none of them appeared to stop him from enjoying life. Amazing!

Have you ever looked at your child and wondered how they see their world? How does it look to them? What do you think? Does it change your perception of life as it did mine?

As for me, it was the beginning of a new awareness. I decided that I was going to look at life with a "glass that is half-full" approach. Was I glad Ryan had a disability? No. Could I change his condition? No. But I realized I could change the way I looked at life.

Life Lesson #1: **Decision time.** As special needs moms, we accept our circumstances. Yes, we wish they were different, but we have a decision to make for ourselves. Do we want to be happy? We need to decide to enjoy our lives, being proactive instead of reactive. By taking control of our attitude, we are in charge of our happiness. Changing our attitude changes the way that we see our future choices as well. We are saying yes to ourselves with this simple decision.

If it has to be a rollercoaster ride, then let go, throw your arms in the air, and scream with delight. "Let's enjoy this ride. Whee!"

What Is Special Needs Grief?

'We're on a mission from God.'

~ Elwood, Blues Brothers Movie

I still remember hearing Ryan's final diagnosis like it was five minutes ago. I bet you remember hearing the shocking news that your child had a disability too. It's something we never forget. When I realized my 9-year-old son would never catch up with the other kids his age my heart broke. Tears were streaming down my face as it all sank in.

We were in new territory and there was no turning back.

While driving to work that day, all I could think about were the DNA test results we had just received. We had waited to go to one of the best facilities in our area to get this test done. We were hoping the DNA test would give us the reason behind his disability, but the results were "inconclusive." Inconclusive meant that Ryan's condition wasn't fixable or explainable. There was no known reason why he was intellectually disabled and developmentally delayed. Period. With that final diagnosis, our story encountered a plot twist that would leave me hanging, or so I thought.

Of course, we asked ourselves—why was this happening, how do we fix this, and was I to blame? Then the time came when there were no more answers. The DNA test results proved to us that we had exhausted our search for answers. The mysteries of life were just that—mysteries. But chalking it up to a mystery didn't make me feel better. (I woke up to the fact that I had to either let it go or buy more aspirin because all this gave me a massive headache.)

With this news, I had to face the inescapable reality that I had no idea what was going to happen to us. Inside I was screaming that I didn't want this. I wanted the life everybody else had! We had not planned for this. All I knew was how to raise normal children.

What happens to us when our child is disabled?

We all land in this same place. We have to face the "special needs grief" that comes with our child's condition.

How Long Does This Last?

Special needs grief begins when you get the shocking news, and it never ends. Every special needs mom agrees she still feels the loss and sadness for what her child will never have, do, or be as they move through life.

The first step was accepting the loss of the normal life we pictured for our first child. Ryan wasn't going to college like his brother. I wouldn't be bragging about my prosperous son like other parents. That special needs grief is about the parents.

Gone is the paint-by-numbers lifestyle that parents envision for their child. Replacing that predictable life is an emptiness and desolation. We are facing the unknown.

The special needs grief, when triggered, sends us back to that empty feeling. Here I go again, as my girlfriend casually complains that her daughter is having boyfriend problems. The regret hits me again wondering how Ryan will ever have a relationship with a woman. I want to empathize with my friends. Yet, I feel sad that Ryan won't have the same natural rite-of-passage life experiences.

Examples are all around us of people who go out of their way to give people with disabilities the same life experiences as the typical person. Tim Tebow's project, *Night to Shine*, (www.TimTebowFoundation.org) gives people with special needs an opportunity to experience a prom. They include all the fun and excitement from getting dressed up to dinner with a date.

Many civic organizations focus on the needs of the disabled, such as the International Optimist Clubs, Best Buddies, Special Olympics, and Kiwanis (check your local chapter for more information).

Life Lesson #2: **Special-needs grief is the end of the dreams you had.** You need to acknowledge the emotions you're feeling, say goodbye to them, and move on.

Labels Are for Soup Cans

'The privilege of a lifetime is being who you are.'
~ Joseph Campbell

Ryan was different from the other kids in his exceptional education classes. He didn't look like he had a disability in any way. He looked like a typical kid. I encounter this today when people wrongly label Ryan as autistic. As his mom, I ask myself when this happens, is it important to correct this blunder or just ignore it? I am not offended, but not all disabled children are autistic. (Yes, I do generally let others know that he is intellectually disabled.)

Does it matter that your child has a specific label attached to his disability? Aren't they unique like each of us, just like snowflakes? While your doctor or school may need to think in those terms, it needs to stay there. We need to think of all children without labels. They are more than people with disabilities—they have unlimited capabilities. There are miracles in their future that we cannot envision.

When I learned Ryan was disabled I couldn't imagine his future. I thought Ryan would be sitting in a corner sucking this thumb for the rest of his life. Today he is more independent, funny, and intuitive than I could have imagined. The future is a mystery. We need to challenge our disabled kids the same way we do our typical kids. Pushing them to do more, be independent, and out of the nest.

Life Lesson #3: **Take no offense.** People make mistakes when guessing your child's diagnosis. We all want to figure people out, and labels help us achieve that. Even other special needs parents get it wrong, so take no offense.

It is easy to assume that people are ignorant, mean, or thoughtless when it comes to disabilities. We feel the need to correct them, to "set them straight." I have fallen into that trap. I was wrong, and my life is immensely better since I resigned from the "social police department."

I see people on Facebook who rant about a slight or snub for the disabled. They ask all their friends to cut-and-paste their editorial comments on their timeline. They want to tell the world how to think, act, or feel. I suggest you don't do it. You're spinning your wheels trying to correct everyone. Turn in your badge and just look the other way.

We all need to clean up our own backyards and leave everyone else alone. Have you heard that there are no rewards for fault-finding and that you should pick your battles? Although these are often overused idioms, I love them, and they do fit many situations. Think about it.

WHY NOT ME?

'Everyone is ignorant, only on different subjects.'

~ Will Rogers

I mistakenly thought we could find the answers to make Ryan like the typical kids. It was disappointing to end our search this way after looking for so long.

After repeatedly pleading with God for a miracle, I finally gave up. I let go. I was wasting my time working on the wrong problem. I changed my prayer to "God, it is all up to you." Why do we end up in the same spot? Funny thing, when we have done all that we can, we plead for God's help. It's backward. The time had come for me to turn it over to God and trust in him.

God didn't fix my son. He was fixing me. He was carrying me until I could find my strength to walk in his shadow under his protection. I had biases about the disabled, and walls of resentment that needed to come down for me to be able to enjoy my new life.

I have a confession… disabled people used to scare me. On our honeymoon, John and I went to dinner at a family-style seafood restaurant. I was looking forward to this meal because I love seafood. Seated behind John was a large family. The father caught my attention when I noticed his blindness. At twenty years old, I hadn't seen blind people without glasses. I thought they all covered their eyes with glasses. I couldn't look away; I was squeamish, and this instantly killed my appetite. It's embarrassing to admit that a blind person shocked me, but to a naïve young woman it was real.

I had the same involuntary and unfortunate reaction that many people have when they see our kids. I was blind, too—to people with disabilities.

Life Lesson #4: **Compassion is a door that swings both ways.** We crave it, and everybody needs it. It's easy to be caught up in the special needs world. We're trying to create a better life for our kids while looking at the ignorance of others with disdain. We just wish they could understand the life we lead. Yet we forget that we all started out ignorant of everything in the disabled world. We are from the "normal" world.

Compassion is what we yearn for, and we forget that everyone else in the world wants it, too. When we are thinking that the other guy should know better, we need to stop right there. We don't know what they are going through either. This extends to our spouses, as well. Processing this life-altering news in your heart isn't always the same as acceptance. It can happen at different levels. We travel at different speeds. Your spouse may need time. We need to help others with compassion for their struggles.

Accept What You Cannot Change

'Sometimes the questions are complicated, and the answers are simple.'

~ Dr. Seuss

Often we see God's plan or purpose so clearly, when we look back on our lives. Why can't we see what is in front of us? If it was so easy and all we had to do was open our eyes, why wouldn't we do it? Seeing God's purpose or plan for our lives begins when we accept that we don't have all the answers, just as I did.

I had to let go of all the dreams and plans that I had for myself, for my family, and for Ryan, and let God take over. There had to be a better plan, because mine wasn't winning any awards. I just had to move out of the way.

My feelings preoccupied me. I didn't know how my husband was processing or grieving this new path. Surely, he was expecting a son who followed in his footsteps as a sports fan and outdoor enthusiast. I should have asked the question, "How are you doing?"

I reached out to God asking him to shape me into the person he needed me to be. I had to start by removing the barriers that were holding me back from finding my purpose and my path. I wanted to be a good mom, wife, and friend. I needed God's help to change my expectation that I could control everything. I saw my security in the people around me and I needed to shift my focus to my higher power, God. It was time to pick up the pieces and look forward to the future with hope.

Life Lesson #5: **Acceptance.** Life with a child with special needs was taking shape. It became my new purpose and plan. My plan is to move the needle towards change, even if it is only one inch. I want to help parents see through the turmoil to achieve a life full of happiness, confidence, and joy. The contribution we are making to the world is meaningful and significant. Most importantly, it *is* your *calling*.

You Are an Exceptional Parent

'Change the way you look at things and the things you look at change.'

~ Wayne Dyer

It's easy to find books that support the everyday mom. But we're here to talk about you, the Exceptional Mom. You are the mom who combines her regular mom duties with her tangled life as a special needs mom. The Exceptional Mom goes beyond the scope of the normal mom with the demands that she must take on.

What makes you an Exceptional Mom? Let's define exceptional: unusual, uncommon, extraordinary, rare, unexpected, outstanding, remarkable, special, and phenomenal. These emotion-packed words describe you and your child with special needs. This is not to brag, boast, or define us as saints. It is who you are, what you will experience, and what you will do together as a parent and child.

I understand the life you're living and the acceptance that you seek without judgment. I have been there, too. That is why I believe you are an Exceptional Mom, the unsung superhero in the disability world. (Superhero capes are coming.)

The challenges we manage would scare most people. You hang in there, ready to do battle with anything and anyone for your child. The parents that I've met along my journey are indeed exceptional. They've stepped up to the challenges and persevered for their child and their family. They recognize they have a unique child in their family and a bond that typical parents will never know or understand. Many parents go beyond their pain and loss. They create foundations, train service dogs, provide yoga for children, develop appropriate childcare programs for churches, and build housing, all for the disabled. We have the opportunity to help one another and pay it forward for the next group of special needs moms.

We need to join with others to make a change. You are part of the solution. *'To whomever much is given, of him will much be required; and to whom much was entrusted, of him more will be asked.'* Luke 12:48WEB

Life Lesson #6: **Perspective.** Now that we've established you as a "super-hero," here are some of your responsibilities. You will see the pain of others, thus increasing your empathy. You will see people struggle to learn, and you will learn patience. You will seek the truth with tact, and gain confidence. Moreover, you will remain calm in the storms, and learn resilience. Being a special needs parent has its rewards that result in your humble and joy-filled life.

Finding Your Support

'For every minute you are angry you lose sixty seconds of happiness.'

~Ralph Waldo Emerson

Finding a family member to babysit was difficult. I considered them my go-to people; they were the ones I trusted most. Okay, I understand most people don't want to take care of a child that was considered a handful. But what if that child was a part of your family?

Before my kids were born, I was happy to help our family when they needed a babysitter for their kids. After Ryan was born, when we needed help, our family wasn't as eager to jump in and return the favor. I thought this was one of the unspoken reciprocal family rules. I watched your kids; now you watch mine. However, it didn't work that way.

A friend shared with me her heartbreaking story of rejection. Her family looks the other way when she needs help with her autistic son. Compounding her despair is the rejection of her son, a member of their family. Sadly, their compassion doesn't extend beyond pity.

My *normal* friends talk about how they are jumping in to help with their typical grandkids. They give the parents opportunities to work or have some time alone. I admit I am jealous. I envy those parents who are lucky enough to have family step in to help.

On the other hand, we are all motivated by our own self-interests. Accordingly, I shouldn't hold it against them because I've been guilty as well.

When researching this topic, I asked other women about their experiences with their families. The older generational moms told their daughters that they had raised their kids, because they were done. They were not available to babysit. Boom! Previous generations pushed their kids out of the nest—you learn to fly, sister, or stay home.

I knew I needed help. My husband needed help, as well, since my career involved travel. I had to be imaginative to solve my childcare needs. When an out-of-town business trip sent me to Atlanta where my grandmother lived, I combined business with a family visit. She played with her great grandson while I worked. We need to be thinking outside the box to find answers to these complex problems.

So how do we make sense of all this without having hard feelings? When juggling our life our emotions are often running on high. We need to accept our friends and family even when they don't jump in to support us in that moment. Talk to your friends and family, tell them what you need, and ask them how they could help you. Developing your support network takes time to find just the right people.

It helped me to separate my circumstances from the source of my frustrations. It's not always the people. That was big. I had to let go of my expectations of others to love them unconditionally. I realized that if their hearts weren't in it to help, then we were all better off.

As an Exceptional Parent, you need to change the way you see your world and the people in it. Creating a life filled with happiness, health, and abundance requires work and this is our mission.

Today there are support groups online and offline to help you and hold your hand. Reach out to them.

Our Story Continues

Life is funny, we think we have it all figured out, then we find out we're wrong. Four years after Ryan was born, along came our son, Christopher. Good news, Christopher was a typical baby; bad news, he was colicky. Of course, we all feel the strain when a new baby arrives. But colicky? Oh, my! He was a crying machine. I couldn't figure out how to comfort him. Our life was chaotic. There was no peace and quiet for anyone anymore.

Life Lesson #7: **Don't Hold a Grudge.** As an Exceptional Mom, you don't have time for anger or hard feelings towards others, you need to try as hard as you can to accept and love others on their own journey. It is impossible to be happy and hold a grudge at the same time. While it would be nice if everyone were available to us when we needed them, it just isn't realistic, so we move on.

Know Yourself Inside And Out

'Every human has four endowments — self-awareness, conscience, independent will, and creative imagination. These give us the ultimate human freedom… The power to choose, to respond, to change.'

~ Stephen Covey

Self-awareness is the essential element to my growth and happiness, and it will be for you, too. It began when I started to look at what triggers my emotions. What makes me see red and charge without thinking into battle? I work on breaking the connection I have with words that will naturally hurt me. The ability to disassociate your feelings from profanity is tough, but useful. I model the positive behavior I see in others and make a choice. Does it always work? No.

'Stick and stones may break my bones, but names will never hurt me' ~ The Christian Recorder

Because the people and situations in our life often become emotional, the better we know ourselves, the better our results. And, I keep trying.

Situation #1

As your child's advocate, you are constantly leading the charge for your child's rights and benefits. You will likely wrestle with your insurance company for benefits or with a government agency for more services at some point. Unfortunately, there are too many opportunities to wrangle with organizations, professionals, and educators for your child. After going round and round with these folks for years, I have found that the better prepared I am, while I remain calm and friendly, the better my results are. I try to think of them as people doing their job and I want to help them reach a resolution that is a win-win for all. To reach the goal I had to control my emotions, not be offended, or be offensive.

Situation #2

The dreaded meltdown is coming. Because our children have a hard time processing their feelings, they will act out. You'll see your child turn into an angry, mean, and hurtful person that you don't recognize. These situations are incredibly hard emotionally, and sometimes even physically. First, you need to keep everyone safe while you weather the storm. Second, when it's over, you need to decompress using healthy methods. Taking a walk, keep moving always helps me.

Think about this *now*, before you're in a crisis. Your child is capable of abusive language and actions that will push all your buttons at once. In any case, pledge that you will be as non-reactive as humanly possible. My son has said things to me that no one would ever say and it is outrageous and despicable. Of course, we can't instinctively react to the tantrum. It would only make matters worse. If this never happens to you, then you will be extremely fortunate. Most of us don't escape.

This is disturbing before, during, and after the fact.

Now is not the time to turn to drugs and alcohol for comfort, although it's an easy choice. Have a plan for yourself and your family. I remind myself that I love my child unconditionally, but I don't have to love what he does.

Learn From My Mistakes

I learned that God never tires of helping me find the right responses to my weaknesses. I found myself comparing my life to the movie, *Groundhog Day*. The character, played by Bill Murray, is doomed to relive the same day repeatedly until he gets it right. While God doesn't make us relive the same day over again (though it may feel that way) he gives us plenty of rope. We need to find and fix our faults.

When I was stuck, I searched everywhere for answers to my problems. I consulted coaches, therapists, friends, family, and even fortune-tellers. I read books, horoscopes, and magazine quizzes. I once went to an astrologer seeking solutions, traveling thirty miles. I learned that the meaning of my astrological sign may be interesting, but it doesn't change my situation.

Nevertheless, my searching continued because I was determined not to be the Eeyore in my own life. You may remember Eeyore from *Winnie the Pooh*. He was the ever-glum, sarcastic, and pessimistic donkey friend to the gang. I wanted to be the Christopher Robin character. The cheerful, compassionate, much wiser, and mature person.

Getting out of your Eeyore rut is the difference between an optimist and a defeatist. Turning your self-limiting beliefs around is a game changer. It all starts when you question what you believe and why. Often I found that my beliefs had nothing to do with the current reality; rather, they were a bias formed from others or through a childhood experience. Once I saw there was no foundation for my belief I started looking for other solutions.

Life Lesson #8: **Be self-aware.** Being stuck can be a good thing. It indicates that it's time for us to learn something new. It's unlikely that you'll be jumping for joy when you realize you're stuck. After you've successfully navigated the challenge, you'll see that you have new resources at your disposal. You will discover that through your self-awareness, you became more resilient and adaptable.

For Better Or Worse?

'Love is patient and is kind; love doesn't envy. Love doesn't brag, is not proud, doesn't behave itself inappropriately, doesn't seek its own way, is not provoked, takes no account of evil; doesn't rejoice in unrighteousness, but rejoices with the truth; bears all things, believes all things, hopes all things, endures all things. Love never fails.'

~ 1 Corinthians 13:4-8WEB

My husband's fairy tale life looked different from mine. He wanted no more than two children and a home with peace and quiet that was far different from his big, noisy family. He knew what it was like to fight, argue, and be near the bottom of the totem pole with four siblings. As an only child, I thought having more than two kids would be wonderful. Fairy tales don't take into account the actual work that is involved in caring for all those kids. That dream would have really been a nightmare for me.

As new parents under pressure, we revert to behaviors we learned in childhood. Remember when your parents demanded to know who broke the 'whatever'? You were under the gun and ready to defend yourself at all costs. Those behaviors worked for a child, but not for adults. We had to learn to be grown-ups.

How Bad Can It Be?

The demands were building on our special family, with workloads and unresponsive family. If only we could have stood back and taken a bigger picture of our situation to see what was really happening. Conflicts would have been easier to resolve if we had only known what the real issues were.

I've heard it said that the secret to a long marriage is that neither person wants to give up and call it quits on the same day. That is true.

Trying to combine the special needs world with the typical began to affect our marriage. It would soon consume our life. We never consciously connected the dots back to the root of our problems.

Life Lesson #9: **Give your partner space**. Marriage in the special needs world has many speed bumps. Under the best of conditions, it is challenging to get on the same page with your spouse. We come from a different background, family style, and emotional stamina. We need to give each other space and time to grow into our Exceptional Parent's roles. We cross these thresholds in our own time with support and love. Don't give up because your partner isn't seeing life the way you do, accept them just as you want to be accepted.

In my mind I'm perfect, except when my husband tries to tell me I'm not, then I either accept or reject his opinion. The key to a long marriage is to have a sense of humor and learn to count (to ten or more).

MARRIAGE 911

'We do the best we can with what we know and when we know better,
we do better.'

~ Maya Angelou

John and I felt like we were juggling balls in the air and tossing them back and forth to each other like hot potatoes. We just didn't have much time to give one another. There were times I felt like his life was easier than mine was because I was doing all the heavy lifting. Of course, that feeling went both ways. We were both dealing with the challenges of being Exceptional Parents. We were doing the best we could. Our hearts went out to our son who couldn't be like everybody else.

We arrived at a point where we were simply out of gas when it came to being a married couple. Our children's lives were consuming us. We weren't the typical overloaded family with soccer, ballet, or T-ball schedules. No. Our schedule included multiple therapy sessions, meetings for school evaluations, and appointments with psychologists. This schedule wasn't optional. It was essential, and we needed to make sure everyone got to his appointments.

When we went out together as a couple, if we didn't talk about the kids, we didn't have much to say. It was an uncomfortable feeling married to a stranger. Where was my friend? I wondered when it happened. When did our relationship splinter off in different directions?

It was a painful and lonely place to be—married, and yet alone.

When relationships get to this point, many couples decide to pull the plug. It can be tough on men, too. They have to process all the special needs grief, just as moms do. Dads typically have buttoned-up feelings. They don't talk about their hurt and pain and why they are detaching from their family. They can't take the burden of the strained marriage and their eroding confidence as a parent, so something has to go, and it's usually the dads. The result is that a man feels like a failure, and he believes he doesn't have any options but divorce.

When we marry, we happily pledge ourselves for better or for worse, until we see how bad it gets. As an Exceptional Parent, we need to understand that failure is never an option. Working together as a couple is far better than going down this road alone.

Typical parents may say their kids are driving them crazy today, yet one day they will be gone. These things even out as the typical child matures and get older. These parents can begin to relax and anticipate taking that nice deep breath of relief. This isn't the case for the Exceptional Mom. By contrast, we need to keep a constant vigil. We need to stay alert to our child's moods, behaviors, or shocking conversations as they mature and grow older.

Life Lesson #10: **Keep your marriage alive.** If you feel like your marriage is slipping away, you need to step back and find a new path. Is your spouse your best friend? He is your partner in this special needs world and the only person who understands what is going on in your home. Remember that you were a couple before you became special needs parents. Keep your relationship growing and thriving with care and attention to detail and to each other.

Starting Over...

'Pain insists upon being attended to. God whispers to us in our pleasures, speaks in our consciences, but shouts in our pains. It is his megaphone to rouse a deaf world'

~ C.S. Lewis

Our life as a couple came back together again in a way I could have never anticipated. We began a side business together at the urging of a friend. The best part of starting this was having common goals and dreams once again. We had something to talk about that didn't include our kids' problems, schedules, or our regular daytime jobs. We were chasing a new dream together, supporting, and encouraging one another. We were building a new bridge between us and it felt good. Travel for the business was fun, as was making new friends and connections, and exploring and laughing again. We also managed to find the support we needed for our kids while we took the time for our business and ourselves.

Spending time together outside of our home in a lighthearted environment changed the way I saw our marriage. I learned to have a sense of humor about life. Most of all, I learned how committed John was to our marriage and to being there for both of his kids. I realized he was up to the challenge of raising both boys, typical and special needs, and building a strong family. I cherished his commitment then, and I still do. Those baby steps continued to build that bridge to a much stronger relationship. Though we don't always agree, we're a committed couple.

Life Lesson #11: **Find your sense of humor**. When life is looking bleak, turn it around with a sense of humor. When people are less fortunate than I am, why should I be so glum and depressed? Find your funny bone. When people say or do something that would normally offend you, turn it around with a joke or a witticism. We grease the gears of life with humor, or as Mary Poppins said, "A spoonful of sugar helps the medicine go down."

What Moms Know That Doctors Don't

'No man should bring children into the world who is unwilling to persevere to the end in their nature and education.'

~ Plato

I remember the day we moved into our new home. Christopher, our four-month-old son, was colicky, Ryan was starting to talk, and we had to move. It was organized chaos. At the same time, Christopher's health got worse because he couldn't keep food down. My attempts to comfort him weren't working. While everyone was carrying boxes out to the moving truck, I was trying to comfort him, and I going crazy. When he began vomiting, I knew it was time for the doctor.

The doctor suggested that we admit him to the hospital, and I was relieved that he would be cared for while I went back to attend to Ryan and the move. Leaving Christopher at the hospital was a tough decision to make. The typical mom would have stayed by her child's side in the hospital.

Nevertheless, the situation progressed from bad to worse. The doctor's grasp of my decision was that I didn't care about my child. Without my knowledge, he called social services to step in and evaluate me. I was furious. I didn't want to leave my child in the hospital, but I had to make a hard choice.

As Exceptional Parents, we all have tough choices to make that others will no doubt question. John was busy with the move, and I had to be sure that Ryan was okay. It all worked out after talking with social services worker who quickly understood the complexities of the situation. Once the day was over and the move was complete, I went back to the hospital to be with Christopher.

Life Lesson #12: **Moms know best**. As a special needs mom, you have the experience from on-the-job training to know when something isn't right with your child. When listening to doctors, instead of thinking that their judgment is absolute, you can judge for yourself. Consider yourself as the second (or third) opinion. Ask for more information.

While doctors do have knowledge from years of training and are life-savers, they haven't walked in your sandals. Every situation is different and unique, and you are your child's advocate. Don't stand back waiting because a doctor tells you it will be okay when your gut tells you differently.

WHO ELSE WANTS MORE TIME?

'Being deeply loved by someone gives you strength while loving someone deeply gives you courage.'

~ Lao Tzu

Do you consider yourself special? I know I was so absorbed in keeping all the plates spinning in my world that I didn't even think about me. I was so busy working, cooking, cleaning, and being a mother, a friend, and a wife that I wasn't including me in the ranking. Have you felt that way? If you stay in that zone for too long, it becomes the red-zone also known as "burnout."

What happens when you suffer burnout? Exhaustion, anxiety, tension, and fatigue are all part of the emotional and physical breakdown that we face. It's inevitable that we're going to find bumps, potholes, walls, mountains, and dead-end paths to our happy place.

Despite our obstacles, we must keep going–we don't have any other choice. Take five minutes everyday for yourself. More is even better, but start with five. Start a list of at least 10 ways to give back, to restore, and rejuvenate yourself.

Life Lesson #13: **You are a priority.** Remember the emergency instructions from the flight attendants. Step one—put the oxygen mask on yourself. Step two—put the mask on your child. Even if you've heard that a million and one times, it still matters. You matter. You matter to everyone. Add yourself to your 'to-do' list.

10 Minutes To A New You

'It's not the load that breaks you down, it's the way you carry it.'

~ Lou Holtz

Move from that place of isolation, loneliness, and hurt to happiness and contentment. Simply apply the methods that so many other Exceptional Parents have learned.

It starts with self-care. If you're an at-home Mom, it's as simple as taking the time to brush your hair, put on clean clothes, moisturize your face, and take your vitamins. I've heard Exceptional Moms say they don't have any time for themselves. I do understand that you put others before your own needs. However, it's all part of putting on your oxygen mask. It's all about the simple little things we need to do for ourselves every day.

Let's not end up a statistic, overloaded and worn out. This is your heads-up. Some Exceptional Moms have figured out how helpful this is, while others are still wondering why they feel drained.

Many community programs offer respite care for parents to enjoy a free afternoon or evening. Never pass those up. Let go of your children and let others help you. During that time, do something for yourself, but do not do your chores! This is not the time to fold the laundry that's been piling up, to mop the floors, or to clean the house. This is the time for you, the Exceptional Mom, to be unabashedly selfish. Use this time to reward yourself and do it even if you don't feel like it.

Life Lesson #14: **Love yourself.** Expanding your morning routine to include 10 minutes for yourself could mean that you'll have to get up earlier to be ahead of the crazy time that's coming. Spend those 10 minutes on your heart. Savor some quiet time, enjoy your coffee, watch the sunrise, or write in your gratitude journal—these are all examples of quality time. This is so important. Rebuild your spirit with the sights, sounds, smells, or touches that make you smile.

How to Build a Friend Network

'Count your age by friends, not years. Count your life by smiles, not tears.'

~ John Lennon

We need friends. We need real-life friends, not the ones you "like" on Facebook. A friend is someone you break bread with, go to the movies with, and share life together.

Today, we're seeing our friends on Facebook and Instagram. Or we're busy messaging, texting, and Skyping them. However, we're missing the critical component that makes a friendship extraordinary.

Our life is lonely and confusing at times and we need someone who isn't shocked by our experiences and who isn't judging us.

I love seeing my friends, sharing my funny stories, and watching their reactions. We're laughing, telling stupid jokes, and talking about what is in our hearts. Each friend feeds my spirit.

I feel alone without my friends. They are like the spritz of lemon in our drink that brings out the brightness and sweet flavor. When we need a kick in the rear, we can count on our friends to give it to us. Friends are always happy to see us, listen to us, support us, and celebrate the joys of life with us. When we're sad, an authentic friend will be there for us.

Here comes the work.

You have to *be* a friend to *have* a friend, and that's what we forget about in our busy, overloaded lives. The truth is we just don't always know what is happening with the people around us, even our closest friends. Our friends may be experiencing pain, or they may have a secret they are afraid to share. We need to be sensitive to their needs and listen to what they are saying and what might be just below the surface. If you want solid friendships, it takes effort.

There's a mutual admiration association among special needs moms for our courage, resilience, and fortitude making those friendships special, as well. They aren't shocked or horrified when we share our latest *breaking news* story from home. Outside of the special needs world, I carefully choose the stories to share with friends. I found that authentic friends care about my life, my family, and my heart. They want to know what's happening in my life. They will never be able to appreciate the complexities that I continue to navigate. They can't appreciate what it's like to teach the same thing again and again until you want to scream. However, they still listen, because they care.

Awkward?

As an Exceptional Parent, I value the limited time I have with friends to relax and enjoy adult conversation. I consider our time together a privilege and don't like sharing it with a cellphone. Let me tell you what happened when I was eating lunch with a work friend.

While eating she took a call on her cellphone from a friend that she talks with daily. While she was busy catching up with the kids' activities, I stopped eating and uncomfortably waited for her to complete her call. Our pleasant lunch just turned into an awkward situation, catching me by surprise.

I considered my options. Should I continue eating by myself, or should I stop and wait for her? Should I pretend to be looking at my phone for something interesting while I wait for her? I was stuck.

I learned that I didn't need that kind of friend. If I wanted to have lunch with her in the future, I had to accept where I ranked in her world.

Life Lesson #15: **Learn to be a friend.** It's not the number of friends that you have as much as the quality of those relationships. When we understand what we like and don't like about our friendships, we then have the responsibility to apply that to ourselves. When your friends don't have time for you, find more friends. I figured out that some of my friends like to meet from time to time, while others like to meet more frequently, so I know which friends to call when I have time. Make it work for you. I have built different groups of friends to keep my life as busy as I want and you can, too. Friends are an important part of life, and each of our friends fills different needs.

Let's roll.

Is Stress Killing You?

'It's like driving a car with your foot on the brake.'

~ Allen Elkin

One of the most destructive aspects of an Exceptional Parent's life is stress. We must be proactive to counteract this threat. A day in the life of the typical mom is overflowing with demands on her time from home, family, and work. If you ask the average mom how she's doing, the usual answer is "busy." Ask an Exceptional Mom how she is doing, and she will answer, "Exhausted."

A Day in My Life

Here's an example from one of my own typical days when the boys were younger. Work was demanding. I had just finished taking Ryan to therapy, and then I was racing through heavy traffic to pick up Christopher at daycare before they closed. Finally, I got home in a frazzled state in time to fix dinner.

There I was, juggling three things at once. The need for dinner was stretching my brain, Christopher was calling out to me for some mysterious reason, and Ryan was in another room by himself.

At that point, I was mentally and physically pooped. I was alone, my husband was at work, and I was in charge. I just wanted to sit down, unwind from the day, and forget about the stress. The strain was building from all the day's activities. My subconscious was continuing to nag at me about all the uncertainties surrounding Ryan's future. I wanted to escape, but of course, I couldn't.

This is the life of the Exceptional Mom. We are constantly turned to "on," the "pause" button is broken, and "off" doesn't operate until we crawl into bed.

Life Lesson #16: **Take Big Belly Breaths.** Identifying techniques to reduce my stress was like finding the pot of gold at the end of the rainbow. I learned that one of the fastest and easiest ways to de-stress is by breathing. Contributing to our tense situation is our poor breathing habits. We hold our breath, or breathe in short, shallow breaths.

I learned that we naturally hold our breath when we are tense or shocked. We use shallow breathing in panic situations. Shallow breathing is our learned state, while taking big belly breaths, just as little babies do, is our natural state. It is also how we breathe during sleep. Start giving your body the much-needed oxygen it needs to release tension with belly breathing. Watch yourself the next time you're stressed, and see how you are breathing.

STRESS WAS MY MIDDLE NAME

'If you're going through hell, keep going.'
~ Winston Churchill said about success

Stress has become a staple of our everyday lives, making it our normal state of being. The truth is our children contribute to our stress with their non-typical annoying characteristics. The fact is that your child is not growing out of that annoying noise they make, or the gesturing, or spinning. It's just who they are, but nonetheless, their actions can be exasperating. There are times their behaviors get on your very last nerve, especially when you're tired and need a few seconds of peace and quiet.

When a fellow special needs mom and I were discussing this, she commented that the moms that deny this truth are liars. There's no need for guilt or shame for your feelings.

Most days I enjoy my son's quirkiness. However, there are times that I wish he weren't so loud, or he didn't walk around the house clapping, or I didn't have to teach him the same thing over again. I know this is the same for all parents—our children push our buttons. However, Exceptional Parents know that this situation isn't going to change, and they're not likely to grow out of this *phase*.

A life full of uncertainty naturally creates tension. The uneasiness simmers below the surface at all times. We love certainty and knowing what's going to happen next. I begin to feel anxious when life becomes unpredictable.

I want life to be like a cupcake recipe. I add the ingredients, stir together, and bake at 350 degrees for thirty minutes to get cute little cupcakes. I like the predictable outcome, the step-by-step and paint-by-the-numbers that everyone else follows. I'm in my comfort zone when life is predictable.

What happens when a new ingredient is added to the recipe? We still have cupcakes, but they don't look or taste the same. Therefore, we try to fix them. We don't understand how this recipe could have changed when we were so careful. Yet, here are our unique cupcakes.

People look at our unique cupcakes, and they don't know how to respond. They want to tell us how sorry they are, but they hesitate because they are not sure if that's the right thing to do. Some people just look and think how lucky they are that those cupcakes don't belong to them.

Without question, we love and accept our kids no matter how wacky they are. We are Exceptional Parents, and we are human. We get tired, too.

Life Lesson #17: **Be honest with yourself.** Admitting that your life and the people in it stink at times is okay. Just because your child has special needs doesn't mean you have to like it. We come to terms with our life, yet there are times when we feel like we have been pushed too far. Let go of your feelings, give yourself permission to unload.

Find a judgment-free zone or someone you feel safe with to share your feelings, or write them down. Even if you just write one word down, it's better than leaving it bottled up inside.

How to Take the Headache Out Of Stress

'You must learn to let go. Release the stress. You were never in control anyway.'

~ Steve Maraboli

The truth is that to survive as an Exceptional Parent we must let go of our stress. Creating a foundation or infrastructure is your secret weapon.

It took me a while to figure this out, and I wish I had known it sooner. That foundation is as simple as planning and organizing your life. This is the elephant you eat, one nibble at a time.

At the post-delivery check-up after our son Christopher was born my doctor asked me how I was doing. I told him the family demands are exhausting. He told me that indeed two children were more than twice the amount of work. (Who knew?)

Know your limitations

We are like everyone else when it comes to the amount of time and energy that we have each day. I want to be with my girlfriends and get together for Bunko, a bible study, or to just hang out.

Over the years, my friends have asked me to host a jewelry, candle, spa, or home party. They always told me how easy and simple it would be to host a party. The truth is, my world isn't simple, and if they knew what was going on in my home, they wouldn't have asked.

Then there was the time that I knew my plate was full and yet I said yes anyway. I started juggling things (people) around so that I didn't drop any of the balls. The result wasn't pretty. I was often late to meetings; I didn't have the time or energy to complete my tasks because I was too busy. On the other hand, I went in the other direction and short-changed my family for my volunteer work.

I was my own worst enemy.

It all starts out so innocently for me. I think I have my family organized, and everything is running smoothly so I take on more responsibilities. Volunteering is my Achilles heel. Before you know it, one minute I'm happy and confident and then my house of cards starts to crumble. I become angry, frustrated, or annoyed with others. The truth is that I only have so much emotional energy, and I can't afford to blow it.

I had created my own stress without realizing it.

Life Lesson #18: **Know your limitations.** It hurts at first to say no when well-meaning friends ask us to help, yet we must weigh the cost to our family and personal well-being. Look for opportunities that match your purpose. Watch out for the 'should-dos', you already have enough of those. Distractions are often shiny objects that look fun but are time wasters. In today's fast-paced world, things are coming at us as if we're standing in front of a fire hydrant with our mouth open when all we wanted was a drink of water.

Need A Kick In The Butt?

'Of course, motivation is not permanent. But then, neither is bathing; but it is something you should do on a regular basis.'

~ Zig Ziglar

While stress is a strain and negatively influences our life, pressure is a force that moves us to make things happen. Pressure is about the urgency of the matter that demands our attention. This definition was illuminating to me.

Let me share a personal example of pressure. Picking a new Support Coordinator for my son was overwhelming me. (This person works on our son's behalf to oversee his services.) The process is confusing, and the state was burdening me to interview as many as two hundred people to find the right person. I stewed about this for a while, mad that I would have to follow their interview process. Who has time to check out two hundred people? The pressure was on. I had no choice; I had to figure this out.

I like simple and effective processes. It was thrilling when I realized I could send all candidates an email explaining what I needed. I gave them specific instructions for applying. Just like a business, I was filling a job vacancy. I was able to cut through the two hundred applicants within a week. Most disqualified themselves when they didn't follow directions, or didn't respond at all.

It worked out beautifully. I was able to use 'pressure' to get the job done. It forced me to streamline the process, put a plan in place, and work that plan.

Think of pressure as your kick-in-the-pants. Do you need to make that phone call you've been avoiding? Do you need to spend time with your spouse, work on yourself, or try a relaxing activity like yoga?

Some of the pressure you feel could be your attempt to force a situation or person, and it isn't working. Letting go of your attempt to control a situation or person is also an option. In every situation, there's a natural push and pull between people. Sometimes an effective solution is just to drop the rope. Give others the freedom to make their own choices, good or bad, consider the outcomes, and just let go.

My son, Ryan, wanted a credit card. He wanted it so bad that he would not quit bugging me about it. This went on for months. He tried to persuade me with everything he had. At the same time, I tried everything I could think of to explain why it was a bad idea. I was attempting to control the situation. I tried to find a solution that would work for everyone. Finally, it occurred to me; give him a prepaid VISA gift card. I could limit the amount of money that would be wasted; yes, I knew that he would blow it, but it's his money. My strategy worked, I dropped the rope and quit struggling. It worked! It was a win-win.

Life Lesson #19: **Sleep on it.** My favorite way to solve problems is to take a nap. I close my eyes, think about the problem, say a prayer, and ask for a solution. Often when I wake up, I have a tidbit in mind that just may be the answer. It could be the missing piece of the puzzle.

When my mind is resting, it works in ways that I wouldn't ordinarily see. My subconscious is running around looking for answers while I'm relaxing.

When dealing with difficult people you must be clear-headed and have a good attitude. Facing problems with confidence knowing that you will find a solution is rewarding. Finding the answers to complex situations requires every trick you can muster.

Time for a high-five.

ADD YEARS TO YOUR LIFE WITH RELAXATION

'It is health that is real wealth and not pieces of gold and silver.'

~ Mahatma Gandhi

Exercising is like work to me. It's something I know I need to do, but I don't always like it. I have to find ways to trick myself to make it seem like fun or a challenge. What I do like about exercising is that it quiets my mind. While I'm sweating or straining, I turn the noise off in my brain. If you're like me, you have those crazy little voices that annoy you, or try to get you to worry. I mentally have to tell them to SHUT UP; it may sound crazy, but it works.

I heard people talking about their love of yoga. Curious, I tried it once and was unsuccessful getting my downward facing dog pose right. I thought standing upside down was silly. However, everyone's infatuation with yoga continued.

My goal was to find something simple to master, easy for a non-athlete. Most of all, I wanted it to work out the tension in my shoulders. So there I went again to check out yoga.

I found that yoga practices and classes are diverse. After trying out a few, I landed on a few places that worked for my schedule, budget, and skill level. If you haven't tried it don't be thrown off by one bad apple, keep looking. You'll find, as I did, that it's almost as good as a massage with a short nap thrown in for good measure. Anything that includes a nap is terrific.

In yoga, I'm learning how to breathe, which is very relaxing in tense situations. Yoga has reduced the pain in my neck and shoulders where I hold my aches and tension. The poses are adaptable for everyone's capabilities.

If you don't have time to leave your home, look for videos on YouTube, DVDs, or websites for yoga poses. Surprisingly yoga is for everyone, including seniors, thanks to chair yoga and gentle yoga. I love stretching. My energy has increased, and I love the sound sleep I have every night, all because I take the time for myself.

If yoga isn't for you, find something else like dancing, biking, or walking. We all need to keep moving to release the tension that naturally builds up from living in the special needs world.

Life Lesson #20: **Say goodbye to tension.** Pick a natural and healthy way to release your tension. Exercise of some kind (including simple stretching every day) will turn your life around. Find an easy to follow routine that you will enjoy and commit to each week. Walking is a simple tension reliever. Studies show that walking 10,000 steps per day (there's a goal) will help keep your weight down along with improving your emotional and mental health. Whatever you can do for yourself is a tremendous gift, and you're worth it. Start small, but just start!

How Do I Manage All This?

'Everybody in the world is seeking happiness – and there is one sure way to find it. That is by controlling your thoughts. Happiness doesn't depend on outward conditions. It depends on inner conditions.'

~ Dale Carnegie, How to Win Friends and Influence People

So Where Do You Go From Here?

Start with yourself. Work on being the best person you can be. Invest in and love yourself. Build a strong foundation that will take you into the future.

Remember you're in a marathon, not a sprint. Give yourself space and time for your journey. You and your family will evolve over time. Often it takes time for those around you to understand and appreciate their role in your family's life. We find that we avoid the angst and anger that springs from disappointment with time. We can't be perfect; neither can we expect those around us to live up to those impossible standards.

Our Children's Future

Their future is a giant question mark! That question mark is where the caregivers step into that special needs world and live. Some survive, some thrive, some flounder, and some just get by. They live their lives for and through someone else, the disabled.

We have the ability to change history for the disabled just as Mothers Against Drunk Drivers, MADD, did when they formed in 1980. The disabled need our help, and they need all hands on deck to make that happen. For those of us that are able to come to their aid, we must come together to find solutions to their problems. And they are big problems.

Each of us can help effect change for the disabled. Find your gifts and use them for the good of those who will never thank you.

Life Lesson #21: **Keep your eyes and ears open.**

The journey in and through the world of the disabled is difficult on all levels. Consider the statement, *"To whomever much is given, of him will much be required; and to whom much was entrusted, of him more will be asked." Luke 12:48 WEB*. This is your assignment; take care with your choices.

Greatness is before you.

For more information about my upcoming books and to get your bonus materials, click on this link: www.ExceptionalParentsPlace.com/BonusMaterials

Life Lessons Summary

Life Lesson #1: **Decision time.** As special needs moms, we accept our circumstances. Yes, we wish they were different, but we have a decision to make for ourselves. Do we want to be happy? We need to decide to enjoy our lives, being proactive instead of reactive. By taking control of our attitude, we are in charge of our happiness. Changing our attitude changes the way that we see our future choices as well. We are saying yes to ourselves with this simple decision.

If it has to be a rollercoaster ride, then let go, throw your arms in the air, and scream with delight. "Let's enjoy this ride. Whee!"

Life Lesson #2: **Special-needs grief is the end of the dreams you had.** You need to acknowledge the emotions you're feeling, say goodbye to them, and move on.

Life Lesson #3: **Take no offense.** People make mistakes when guessing your child's diagnosis. We all want to figure people out, and labels help us achieve that. Even other special needs parents get it wrong, so take no offense.

It is easy to assume that people are ignorant, mean, or thoughtless when it comes to disabilities. We feel the need to correct them, to "set them straight." I have fallen into that trap. I was wrong, and my life is immensely better since I resigned from the "social police department."

I see people on Facebook who rant about a slight or snub for the disabled. They ask all their friends to cut-and-paste their editorial comments on their timeline. They want to tell the world how to think, act, or feel. I suggest you don't do it. You're spinning your wheels trying to correct everyone. Turn in your badge and just look the other way.

We all need to clean up our own backyards and leave everyone else alone. Have you heard that there are no rewards for fault-finding and that you should pick your battles? Although these are often overused idioms, I love them, and they do fit many situations. Think about it.

Life Lesson #4: **Compassion is a door that swings both ways**. We crave it, and everybody needs it. It's easy to be caught up in the special needs world. We're trying to create a better life for our kids while looking at the ignorance of others with disdain. We just wish they could understand the life we lead. Yet we forget that we all started out ignorant of everything in the disabled world. We are from the "normal" world.

Compassion is what we yearn for, and we forget that everyone else in the world wants it, too. When we are thinking that the other guy should know better, we need to stop right there. We don't know what they are going through either. This extends to our spouses, as well. Processing this life-altering news in your heart isn't always the same as acceptance. It can happen at different levels. We travel at different speeds. Your spouse may need time. We need to help others with compassion for their struggles.

Life Lesson #5: **Acceptance.** Life with a child with special needs was taking shape. It became my new purpose and plan. My plan is to move the needle towards change, even if it is only one inch. I want to help parents see through the turmoil to achieve a life full of happiness, confidence, and joy. The contribution we are making to the world is meaningful and significant. Most importantly, it *is* your *calling*.

Life Lesson #6: **Perspective.** Now that we've established you as a "super-hero," here are some of your responsibilities. You will see the pain of others, thus increasing your empathy. You will see people struggle to learn, and you will learn patience. You will seek the truth with tact, and gain confidence. Moreover, you will remain calm in the storms, and learn resilience. Being a special needs parent has its rewards that result in your humble and joy-filled life.

Life Lesson #7: **Don't Hold a Grudge.** As an Exceptional Mom, you don't have time for anger or hard feelings towards others, you need to try as hard as you can to accept and love others on their own journey. It is impossible to be happy and hold a grudge at the same time. While it would be nice if everyone were available to us when we needed them, it just isn't realistic, so we move on.

Life Lesson #8: **Be self-aware.** Being stuck can be a good thing. It indicates that it's time for us to learn something new. It's unlikely that you'll be jumping for joy when you realize you're stuck. After you've successfully navigated the challenge, you'll see that you have new resources at your disposal. You will discover that through your self-awareness, you became more resilient and adaptable.

Life Lesson #9: **Give your partner space**. Marriage in the special needs world has many speed bumps. Under the best of conditions, it is challenging to get on the same page with your spouse. We come from a different background, family style, and emotional stamina. We need to give each other space and time to grow into our Exceptional Parent's roles. We cross these thresholds in our own time with support and love. Don't give up because your partner isn't seeing life the way you do, accept them just as you want to be accepted.

In my mind I'm perfect, except when my husband tries to tell me I'm not, then I either accept or reject his opinion. The key to a long marriage is to have a sense of humor and learn to count (to ten or more).

Life Lesson #10: **Keep your marriage alive.** If you feel like your marriage is slipping away, you need to step back and find a new path. Is your spouse your best friend? He is your partner in this special needs world and the only person who understands what is going on in your home. Remember that you were a couple before you became special needs parents. Keep your relationship growing and thriving with care and attention to detail and to each other.

Life Lesson #11: **Find your sense of humor**. When life is looking bleak, turn it around with a sense of humor. When people are less fortunate than I am, why should I be so glum and depressed? Find your funny bone. When people say or do something that would normally offend you, turn it around with a joke or a witticism. We grease the gears of life with humor, or as Mary Poppins said, "A spoonful of sugar helps the medicine go down."

Life Lesson #12: **Moms know best**. As a special needs mom, you have the experience from on-the-job training to know when something isn't right with your child. When listening to doctors, instead of thinking that their judgment is absolute, you can judge for yourself. Consider yourself as the second (or third) opinion. Ask for more information.

While doctors do have knowledge from years of training and are life-savers, they haven't walked in your sandals. Every situation is different and unique, and you are your child's advocate. Don't stand back waiting because a doctor tells you it will be okay when your gut tells you differently.

Life Lesson #13: **You are a priority.** Remember the emergency instructions from the flight attendants. Step one—put the oxygen mask on yourself. Step two—put the mask on your child. Even if you've heard that a million and one times, it still matters. You matter. You matter to everyone. Add yourself to your 'to-do' list.

Life Lesson #14: **Love yourself.** Expanding your morning routine to include 10 minutes for yourself could mean that you'll have to get up earlier to be ahead of the crazy time that's coming. Spend those 10 minutes on your heart. Savor some quiet time, enjoy your coffee, watch the sunrise, or write in your gratitude journal—these are all examples of quality time. This is so important. Rebuild your spirit with the sights, sounds, smells, or touches that make you smile.

Life Lesson #15: **Learn to be a friend.** It's not the number of friends that you have as much as the quality of those relationships. When we understand what we like and don't like about our friendships, we then have the responsibility to apply that to ourselves. When your friends don't have time for you, find more friends. I figured out that some of my friends like to meet from time to time, while others like to meet more frequently, so I know which friends to call when I have time. Make it work for you. I have built different groups of friends to keep my life as busy as I want and you can, too. Friends are an important part of life, and each of our friends fills different needs.

Let's roll.

Life Lesson #16: **Take Big Belly Breaths.** Identifying techniques to reduce my stress was like finding the pot of gold at the end of the rainbow. I learned that one of the fastest and easiest ways to de-stress is by breathing. Contributing to our tense situation is our poor breathing habits. We hold our breath, or breathe in short, shallow breaths.

I learned that we naturally hold our breath when we are tense or shocked. We use shallow breathing in panic situations. Shallow breathing is our learned state, while taking big belly breaths, just as little babies do, is our natural state. It is also how we breathe during sleep. Start giving your body the much-needed oxygen it needs to release tension with belly breathing. Watch yourself the next time you're stressed, and see how you are breathing.

Life Lesson #17: **Be honest with yourself.** Admitting that your life and the people in it stink at times is okay. Just because your child has special needs doesn't mean you have to like it. We come to terms with our life, yet there are times when we feel like we have been pushed too far. Let go of your feelings, give yourself permission to unload.

Find a judgment-free zone or someone you feel safe with to share your feelings, or write them down. Even if you just write one word down, it's better than leaving it bottled up inside.

Life Lesson #18: **Know your limitations.** It hurts at first to say no when well-meaning friends ask us to help, yet we must weigh the cost to our family and personal well-being. Look for opportunities that match your purpose. Watch out for the 'should-dos', you already have enough of those. Distractions are often shiny objects that look fun but are time wasters. In today's fast-paced world, things are coming at us as if we're standing in front of a fire hydrant with our mouth open when all we wanted was a drink of water.

Life Lesson #19: **Sleep on it.** My favorite way to solve problems is to take a nap. I close my eyes, think about the problem, say a prayer, and ask for a solution. Often when I wake up, I have a tidbit in mind that just may be the answer. It could be the missing piece of the puzzle.

When my mind is resting, it works in ways that I wouldn't ordinarily see. My subconscious is running around looking for answers while I'm relaxing.

When dealing with difficult people you must be clear-headed and have a good attitude. Facing problems with confidence knowing that you will find a solution is rewarding. Finding the answers to complex situations requires every trick you can muster.

Time for a high-five.

Life Lesson #20: **Say goodbye to tension.** Pick a natural and healthy way to release your tension. Exercise of some kind (including simple stretching every day) will turn your life around. Find an easy to follow routine that you will enjoy and commit to each week. Walking is a simple tension reliever. Studies show that walking 10,000 steps per day (there's a goal) will help keep your weight down along with improving your emotional and mental health. Whatever you can do for yourself is a tremendous gift, and you're worth it. Start small, but just start!

Life Lesson #21: **Keep your eyes and ears open.**

The journey in and through the world of the disabled is difficult on all levels. Consider the statement, *"To whomever much is given, of him will much be required; and to whom much was entrusted, of him more will be asked." Luke 12:48WEB.* This is your assignment; take care with your choices.

Greatness is before you.

I HOPE YOU HAVE ENJOYED THIS BOOK......

I hope that you have enjoyed this book and have some new steps that you will consider and implement. Most of all, I hope that you will find your own path to your Happy Place. Look around you and bring some other moms along with you.

Post a Review on Amazon

Let your friends and family know what you liked in the book with a review. Your reviews are important, so I thank you in advance for taking the time to share your thoughts with others.

Contact me with your thoughts or suggestions for future topics that you would like to read about.

Take time for yourself; remember you are worth it!